# THE STORY OF AUDREY HEPBURN

T0008811

## An Inspiring Biography for Young Readers

— Written by —
**Natasha Wing**

— Illustrations by —
**Marta Dorado**

callisto
publishing
an imprint of Sourcebooks

{ To the women in my life, who
are beautiful inside and out. }

Copyright © 2024 by Callisto Publishing LLC
Cover and internal design © 2024 by Callisto Publishing LLC
Illustrations © Marta Dorado with the following exception:
© Semicircular/Creative Market (maps)
Photographs by Alamy: © Pictorial Press Ltd: 49; © AA Film Archive/Allstar Picture Library Ltd: 50;
© marka/Universal Images Group North America LLC: 52
Author photo courtesy of Richard Mauro Ricchiuti
Series Designer: Angela Navarra
Art Director: Angela Navarra
Art Producer: Stacey Stambaugh
Editor: Kristen Depken
Production Editor: Rachel Taenzler
Production Manager: Martin Worthington

Library of Congress Cataloging-in-Publication data is on file with the publisher.

This product conforms to all applicable CPSC and CPSIA standards.

Source of Production: Versa Press
Date of Production: March 2024
Run Number: 5038721

Printed and bound in the United States of America.
VP 10 9 8 7 6 5 4 3 2 1

# CONTENTS

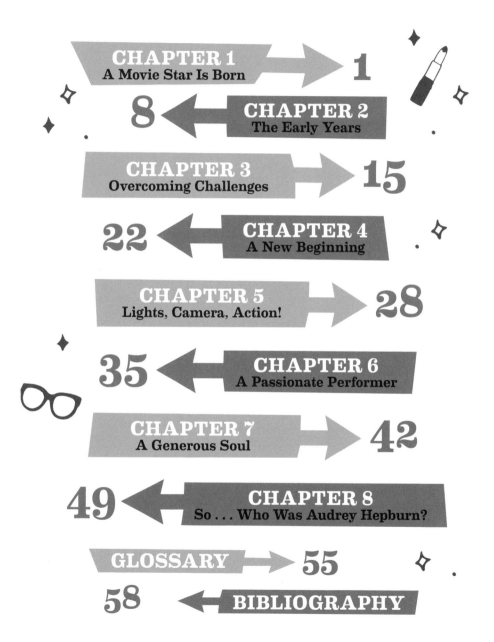

# CHAPTER 1

# A MOVIE STAR IS BORN

# ✦ Meet Audrey Hepburn ✦

Audrey Hepburn was one of the most beloved actresses in America. She first stole Americans' hearts when she starred in the Broadway play *Gigi*. Then she won an important film award called an Oscar for Best Actress in the movie *Roman Holiday*. Audrey went on to star in plays, movies, and television shows. She is one of 18 artists who have earned a special combination of four awards given for television, music, film, and stage performances.

Audrey was adored by fans, fashion designers, and fellow actors around the world. She was also adored by a deer she starred with in a movie. Pippin followed her everywhere. She even took her pet deer shopping!

Yet behind Audrey's big brown eyes, she hid her pain. As talented as she was, she hadn't planned on being an actress. Her dream was

to be a ballerina. Her dance lessons and performances ended up helping her in Hollywood. She did her own dancing in movies.

Later in life, Audrey became a Goodwill **Ambassador** for **UNICEF**. This means she went all over the world to represent them. UNICEF takes care of sick and starving children who are victims of war. Audrey knew what it was like to be hungry. She grew up during a war, when food was hard to come by. UNICEF delivered food to Europe. It saved children like Audrey from starving.

Audrey lived her life with grace and gratitude. She knew that kindness could help children just like her!

## ✦ Audrey's World ✦

Audrey Kathleen Ruston was born May 4, 1929, in Ixelles, Belgium to Joseph and Ella Ruston. She had two older half brothers. When she was only 21 days old, Audrey turned blue from whooping cough, a disease that makes it hard to breathe. Her mother turned her upside down and spanked her bottom. Audrey could breathe again! But later, she'd have trouble breathing because of **asthma**.

JUMP
—IN THE—
THINK
TANK

Audrey dreamed of being a ballerina, but she grew up to be a famous actress. What do you dream of being?

WHERE?

IXELLES

BELGIUM

FRANCE

> " Nothing is impossible. The word itself says 'I'm possible'! "

The year Audrey was born, a **depression** began. In the United States, it was called the Great Depression. It was hard to find jobs and food. People were asking their countries to protect them and give them a better life. In Europe, Adolf Hitler was a new leader of Germany. He promised to make his country strong again. Many Germans trusted Hitler. They believed he would help Germany. But in

time, the world found out Hitler was an evil **dictator** filled with hatred for Jewish people.

Audrey and her family moved to the Netherlands. It is a country known for its windmills and rich soil. Farmers plant tulip bulbs that bloom into fields of colorful tulips. At one time, Audrey ate tulip bulbs to stay alive.

In America, the golden years of Hollywood began during the Great Depression. Movie stars dressed in fancy clothes and diamonds. As a teenager, Audrey once had to wear her brother's shoes and dress in clothes made from curtains. But one day she would become a fashion **icon** in Hollywood. She'd make the little black dress famous.

Women gain the right to vote in every state in the U.S.

**1920**

Audrey's parents get married.

**1926**

Audrey Kathleen Ruston is born.

**1929**

The Great Depression begins.

**1929**

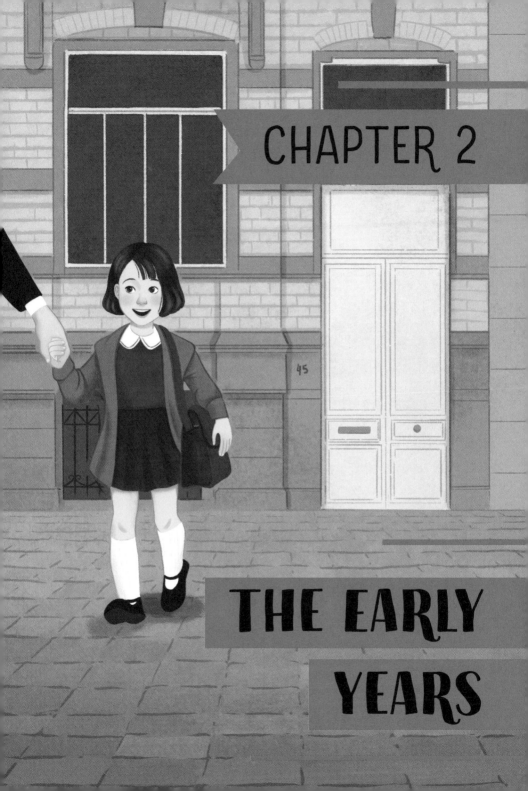

CHAPTER 2

THE EARLY YEARS

# ✦ Growing Up in Belgium ✦

Before Audrey's mom met her dad, she was married to an oilman. Ella van Hemmstra and her first husband had two sons, Alexander and Ian. After five years, they divorced, and Ella met her new husband, John Ruston.

John was English. His family had money, but he did not. He was hoping he had married into a rich family. After all, Ella was a **baroness**. But Ella's family didn't have a lot of money. Ella and John loved each other and got married anyway.

Baroness Ella had a strong personality and an independent spirit. When she found out her husband was related to an English nobleman named James Hepburn, she was very proud. She told John to add Hepburn to their last name.

John, Ella, Alexander, and Ian lived in Ixelles, Belgium. It was part of the capital city, Brussels. Audrey was born there a few years later.

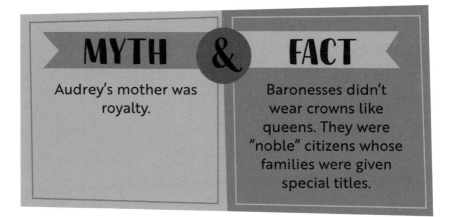

| MYTH | & | FACT |
|------|---|------|
| Audrey's mother was royalty. | | Baronesses didn't wear crowns like queens. They were "noble" citizens whose families were given special titles. |

The family called her Adriaantje. Audrey adored her father. He taught her how to read and write. He showed her how to ride horses. He took her flying in his glider plane. She craved his attention, especially when he came home after a long time away. Her older half brothers loved their baby sister. They'd play outside, climbing trees. Around them, she wasn't shy or quiet!

Audrey's life at home was hard. Her parents fought over money. The family lived in Brussels, but her father worked in London. When her parents traveled, the kids stayed at their grandparents' house in the Netherlands. Audrey called them Opa and Oma. She didn't like

## Audrey's Family

VICTOR JOHN GEORGE RUSTON
1860?-1940

ANNA JULIANA FRANZISKA KAROLINA WELLS
1868-1890

AARNOUD JAN ANNE ALEID, BARON VAN HEEMSTRA
1871-1957

ELBRIG WILLEMINE HENRIETTE, BARONESS VAN ASBECK
1873-1939

AUDREY
1929-1993

JOSEPH RUSTON
1889-1980

ELLA VAN HEEMSTRA
1900-1984

ALEXANDER QUARLES VAN UFFORD
1920-1979

IAN EDGAR BRUCE QUARLES VAN UFFORD
1924-2010

moving around so much. She wanted to stay in one place that felt like home.

## ✦ Discovering Dance in England ✦

Things at home got worse. Audrey's parents were traveling even more. When they were home, they were fighting. Audrey was sensitive, and the fighting made her anxious. She also had asthma attacks.

In Germany, people were looking for a strong leader to make things better. Adolf Hitler promised to fix the country's problems. His group, called **Nazis,** believed Germans were better than other people. They wanted to destroy people who were different, including Jews and people with disabilities. Hitler built up the military so Germany could have more power.

John and Ella approved of Hitler's attempt to pull Germany out of the depression. John even left his family to work with a group in London.

It supported Hitler's ideas. Audrey felt abandoned.

Because he had grown up in England, Audrey's father demanded that she go to school there, too. She was sent hundreds of miles away to a private boarding school in Elham, a small village in the countryside. She was six years old and in a new country, far away from her brothers. Audrey joined a Brownie troop and made some friends. She also bonded with her music and English teacher. When Audrey was about eight years old, the teacher encouraged her to try dance. A ballerina from London came once a week and gave ballet classes. Audrey loved it! She stayed in London and began taking music and ballet lessons.

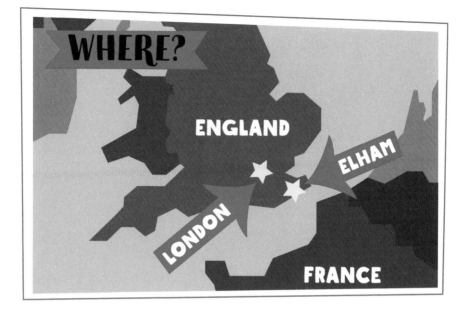

ENGLAND

ELHAM

LONDON

FRANCE

## WHEN?

| Adolf Hitler becomes dictator of Germany. | John leaves the family. | Audrey is sent to boarding school in England. | Audrey starts to take music and ballet lessons. |
|---|---|---|---|
| **1933** | **1935** | **1935** | **1935** |

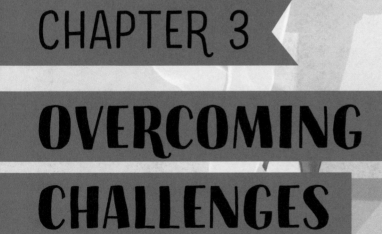

# CHAPTER 3

# OVERCOMING CHALLENGES

# ✦ War Begins ✦

While Audrey was in England, her mother and brothers moved to the Netherlands. They lived with Ella's parents. Oma was very sick and needed family care. In 1938, Germany started invading other countries. On September 3, 1939, Great Britain and France declared war on Germany. It was the start of World War II. The United States joined the war against Germany in 1941. Inside Germany, the Nazis were killing Jewish people.

Ella was afraid Germany would bomb England, so Audrey's father put Audrey on the last plane out of London. She reunited with her mother and brothers in the city of Arnhem, where they thought it would be safe. Audrey's parents had divorced, so her father stayed in England.

The language spoken in the Netherlands is called Dutch. Now that England was Hitler's enemy, Ella changed Audrey's name to Edda.

She thought Edda sounded more Dutch than English, so Audrey would be safer. "Edda" attended a new school. Everyone spoke Dutch except her. Children made fun of her accent and made her cry. But Audrey was gifted at languages. She learned Dutch quickly. By the time she grew up, Audrey spoke at least six languages.

Audrey found peace in the outdoors. She loved flowers and being among the trees. She dreamed of one day having her own country garden. Ella worried about Audrey. One night, she took her to a show to cheer her up. Audrey loved how the ballet dancers moved to the music. She asked to take ballet lessons again, and her mother agreed. Audrey loved ballet so much that she decided to be a ballerina when she grew up.

## **Helping Others ✦ in Hard Times ✦**

**JUMP —IN THE— THINK TANK**

Audrey had to change her name to stay safe. If you could change your name, what would you pick?

One day, Audrey was on stage handing flowers to the head of a dance company. The next day, Germany invaded the Netherlands. War planes flew overhead.

Cannons boomed. Sirens sounded. People hid in their cellars. At first, Ella was friendly with the Germans. She even had Audrey dance for German soldiers. But as Germany became more violent toward Jewish people, Ella began to question the Nazis' ideas. Audrey's half brother Ian was sent to Germany to work in a factory. Her other half brother, Alex, went into hiding rather than join the German forces. What was left of the family moved to the city of Velp. Then one day, Audrey's Uncle Otto, her mother's brother, was arrested, and later killed.

By now, Ella no longer supported Hitler. The family joined the Dutch **Resistance** to fight against him. Audrey helped wounded **Allied** soldiers. She tucked secret messages into her shoes and delivered them by bicycle. She held illegal dance performances to raise money for the Resistance. Guards stood outside to warn them if German soldiers were nearby. Audrey's grandfather hid a British fighter in the cellar of the family home. If the Germans found out the family was helping the **Dutch Underground**, they would be in danger. Even so, the family refused to give up. To fill her days, Audrey taught dance. People thanked her for lifting their spirits during the gloom of war.

Food became more scarce. People dug up whatever they could find in fields. They boiled potatoes to make broth and ground up brown beans for bread. They dug up and ate tulip bulbs. Audrey got skinny. Soon she was too weak to dance.

In 1945, Allies fought off the Germans. The war was over! Audrey was so happy.

But she always remembered how hard the war was for her and her family.

> 66 I still feel sick when
> I remember the scenes. 99

## WHEN?

| Audrey's grandmother, or Oma, dies. | Audrey's parents divorce. | WWII begins. |
|---|---|---|
| **1939** | **1939** | **1939** |
| Audrey moves to Arnhem. | Germany invades the Netherlands. | WWII ends. |
| **1939** | **1940** | **1945** |

# CHAPTER 4
## A NEW
## BEGINNING

# ✦ From Dancing to Acting ✦

After the war, trucks delivered food, medicine, and clothes to help people get back on their feet. Audrey picked out new clothes and ate chocolate until her stomach hurt.

Audrey still wanted to become a **prima ballerina**. She and her mom moved to Amsterdam, where Audrey studied ballet. To earn money, Audrey worked as a model. She also got a small part in a travel movie about the Netherlands. The filmmakers loved how she moved with the grace of a dancer. They loved her smile! But Audrey didn't think she was much of an actress.

She hoped to get a **scholarship** with Marie Rambert's famous ballet school. She worked hard to get ready for her **audition**. She got in and began studying with a ballet **legend**.

Audrey worked hard, but her body just wasn't right for a prima ballerina. Back then, ballerinas were expected to look a certain way. Audrey's neck was too long and her feet were too big. She was taller than the other girls. Because food was scarce during the war, her muscles hadn't grown properly. Audrey's ballet teacher told her she would never be a prima ballerina.

She'd have to find other ways to make money. She tried acting in musicals. Around this time, she dropped "Ruston" from her last name. From now on her name would be Audrey Hepburn.

## JUMP
### —IN THE—
## THINK TANK

If you could act on stage, what kind of show would you be in? A musical? A comedy? Or a serious play?

23

## ✦ A Stunning Stage Debut ✦

Thousands of dancers tried out for the musical *High Button Shoes*. There were ten openings, and Audrey got one of them. She made her stage debut as a **chorus girl**. She had one line.

A **producer** for another musical saw Audrey perform. He hired her for a small role. At the same time, Audrey discovered **cabaret**. Each night when the musical ended, she changed clothes and performed in two cabaret shows that started at midnight. During the day, she modeled and filmed small parts for television shows.

Audrey took an acting class to improve her skills. The class taught her how to **project** her voice and clearly say each word. She also learned how to react to other actors saying their lines.

Finally, she got her first important movie role. She played a ballerina in the musical *Secret People*. Audrey did her own dances in the movie, which most actors didn't do.

Audrey's big break came when she was cast in the title role in a play called *Gigi*. She was 22 years old when she went to

New York City to star in the hit Broadway play. Audiences loved her, and she won her first award for a stage performance.

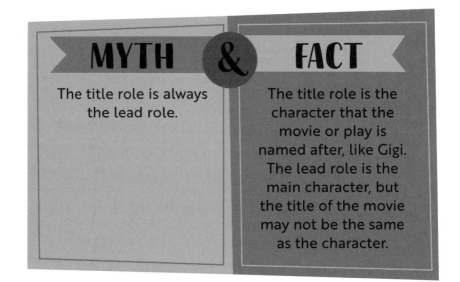

# MYTH & FACT

**MYTH**

The title role is always the lead role.

**FACT**

The title role is the character that the movie or play is named after, like Gigi. The lead role is the main character, but the title of the movie may not be the same as the character.

# WHEN?

| Audrey is in her first film. | Audrey is a chorus girl in *High Button Shoes.* | Audrey plays the title role in *Gigi.* | *Secret People* is released. |
| --- | --- | --- | --- |
| **1948** | **1948** | **1951** | **1952** |

# CHAPTER 5

# LIGHTS, CAMERA, ACTION!

# ✦ An Award-Winning Actress ✦

Audrey had lots of promise and personality. Audiences thought she was refreshing and funny. The features that made her look different, such as her long neck, also made her special. The camera loved her! And so did her fans.

An award-winning **director** needed a lead actress for his new film. It was a romantic comedy called *Roman Holiday*. Audrey was not

his first choice. He wanted a famous actress named Elizabeth Taylor to play the princess in his movie. But Audrey's audition caught the director's eye. He hired Audrey for the role. *Roman Holiday* changed Audrey's life.

## JUMP —IN THE— THINK TANK

Audrey got to travel to Rome to film *Roman Holiday*. Where would you like to film a movie?

Audrey shined in her first starring role in a major film. She even outshined Gregory Peck, one of the world's biggest male stars at the time. Gregory was supposed to get top billing in the movie. He wanted to share it with Audrey instead. He thought she would win an Oscar in her first performance. And she did!

*Roman Holiday* was a huge success. Audrey won three major awards for Best Actress: an Academy Award (also called an Oscar), a BAFTA (British Academy of Film and Television Arts) award, and a Golden Globe.

People in the film industry loved Audrey because she was hardworking. She was always prepared and knew her lines. She was also humble, funny, and kind. Many people, especially women and girls, looked up to her. Suddenly, Audrey's face was everywhere: in movies, on **playbills** for Broadway plays, and on the front covers of magazines.

## ✦ A Fashion Icon ✦

Audrey went from being a girl who owned few clothes and wore her brother's shoes to being a major fashion **influencer**. She had a strong sense of what looked good on her. She also understood how clothes helped create her characters when she acted.

Audrey wanted a fashion designer to style her clothes for a new movie. She went to Paris to meet with a famous designer named Hubert de Givenchy. Hubert was expecting another movie star, Katharine Hepburn. The two women had

the same last name, but they were not related. When Audrey Hepburn showed up in pants, a white cropped T-shirt, a straw hat, and ballerina flats, he tried to send her away. She charmed him into letting her try on some of the clothes he designed. He saw her go from a plain woman to a breathtaking beauty! Hubert became her designer and friend until the end of her life.

Hubert created the clothes Audrey wore in movies and in her everyday life. Her style became known as the Audrey look. It was simple and **elegant**, just like the little black dress she made famous in the movie *Breakfast at Tiffany's*. This dress is still one of the most famous movie costumes.

While Hollywood stars wore fancy dresses, Audrey preferred to wear comfortable clothes. She liked white button-down men's shirts with cropped pants and flat shoes instead of high heels. It was an easy style that any woman could wear. She believed that happy girls were the prettiest girls, so why not be comfortable? Even today, women around the world wear the Audrey look. Designers still celebrate her timeless style.

**Clothes are positively a passion with me.**

# WHEN?

|  |  |  |
|---|---|---|
| *Roman Holiday* is filmed in Italy. | Audrey meets Hubert de Givenchy. | Audrey wins an Oscar for her first starring role in a movie. |
| **1952** | **1953** | **1954** |

# CHAPTER 6

# A PASSIONATE PERFORMER

# ✦ Continued Success ✦

It seemed that Audrey Hepburn could do it all. She acted in plays, television shows, and movies. She starred in a range of film **genres**, including romantic comedies, musicals like *My Fair Lady,* and serious thrillers and dramas. Audrey played a variety of roles: a blind woman, a princess, a girl living in the forest, and a nun. She was **nominated** for five Academy Awards!

But her most beloved and memorable movie role was Holly Golightly in *Breakfast at Tiffany's.* Holly, a kooky New York party girl, falls in love with a struggling writer. In the opening scene, she wore a black dress, gloves, pearls, and sunglasses, and she stole the show. She was nominated for an Oscar for Best Actress. The song she sang in the movie, "Moon River," won an Oscar for Best Original Song.

In 1954, Audrey made her last appearance on Broadway. She played a fairy named Ondine, which was also the name of the play. She won a Tony Award for her performance. Audrey's most special career achievement was earning an EGOT: an Emmy Award for television, a Grammy Award for music, an Oscar for film, and a Tony Award for theater. Only 18 artists have done that.

But Audrey did not let fame go to her head. She was always humble, downplaying her talent and saying nice things about her fellow actors. She was forever grateful for the good things that came her way. She didn't have the training like other actors, and she had stage fright every time she went on stage. But she worked hard. Dance had taught her that if she could feel a

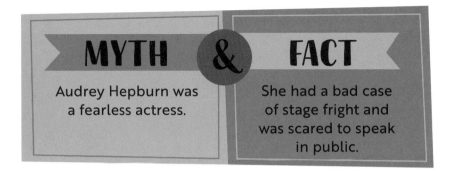

character from the inside, those feelings would show on stage and in film.

## Family and Furry Friends

Because Audrey had an absent father, having a family of her own was important to her. She longed for children to love with all her heart. Audrey was married twice, once to Mel Ferrer, an American actor, and then a second time to Andrea Dotti, an Italian doctor. Both marriages ended in divorce, but she had two sons. Sean was born in 1960 and Luca in 1970.

Both children were born in Switzerland.
Audrey kept them grounded by living in Europe
instead of under the spotlight of Hollywood.
Audrey preferred a quiet life in the country with
her sons, dogs, and gardens. She continued to act
but now chose movies she could work on while
her kids were in school. Sometimes she'd bring

Sean to the set. Other times she'd turn down movies so she could be with her family.

Audrey loved animals, too. She bonded with Pippin the deer on a movie set. She adored dogs and had poodles, terriers, and a boxer. She called them little hamburgers! She once said she couldn't think of anything happier than cuddling and playing with a warm puppy.

JUMP
–IN THE–
THINK
TANK

Audrey had a lot of dogs. What pet do you have? What pet would you like to have?

One Yorkshire terrier, Mr. Famous, went with her on bike rides, plane trips, photo shoots, and movie sets. He was even in a movie! At a movie premiere, Audrey wore a gown and gloves and had two poodles by her side. Audrey was one of the first actors to bring a dog along wherever she went. She was seen and photographed with dogs so much that she made furry friends fashionable.

## WHEN?

Audrey wins a Tony Award for Best Actress in *Ondine*.

Audrey is the lead in *The Nun's Story*.

Sean Hepburn Ferrer is born.

**1954**

**1959**

**1960**

Audrey stars in *Breakfast at Tiffany's*.

Luca Dotti is born.

**1961**

**1970**

CHAPTER 7

A GENEROUS SOUL

# ✦ Compassion for Others ✦

Even when she was a little girl, Audrey loved children. She also knew the pain of hunger from the war. As a mother, she felt it was her duty to help mothers and children who were victims of war.

By 1988, Audrey had **retired** from acting. Now she could use her star power in a new way, as a Goodwill Ambassador for UNICEF. The organization began after World War II to help children. Audrey remembered what it was like to receive food and medicine after the war. The people who helped her inspired her to work with UNICEF. As an ambassador, Audrey traveled to countries suffering from war. Audrey wasn't afraid to go to war zones and help others.

On her first trip, she traveled to Ethiopia, a country in Africa. She visited an **orphanage** filled with children. Audrey visited Guatemala to help people get drinking water. She visited a **vaccine** project in Turkey. For her last trip, in 1992, Audrey traveled to Somalia to show the world the poor living conditions there. People listened to Audrey and gave money to UNICEF to help.

# JUMP
## —IN THE—
# THINK TANK

Audrey wished there were a college where people could learn about peace. What kind of classes do you think a college like that would have?

Audrey spoke to **Congress**, at events, and to reporters about how UNICEF helped people. Whenever she spoke, people raised money. In her four years as ambassador, she took 50 UNICEF trips and raised millions of dollars. Thanks to Audrey's work, UNICEF helped even more poor children around the world.

# ✦ Audrey's Legacy ✦

Audrey was a brave person. She survived a war. She became an actress despite stage fright. She wasn't afraid to be herself and start new fashion trends. And she put children in need over her own safety. She wished she could do more for UNICEF, but she was tired. For the last few years of her life, she felt a pain that worried her. By the time the doctors knew she was sick, it was too late. She spent her last Christmas with her family, then died at age 63.

Audrey is remembered as a fashion icon. People still dress like her today. Her movies are beloved. In 1999, the American Film Institute ranked Audrey as the third-greatest female screen legend of all time. Her many awards prove it! Audrey was also a loving mother to her two sons. She doted on her dogs. And she gave her love freely to the children of the world.

President George H. W. Bush gave Audrey the Presidential Medal of Freedom. This is a special award given to someone who has worked to make the United States a better place. She also received the Jean Hersholt Humanitarian Award. It is given to a person in the film industry for their **humanitarian** work. Outside the UNICEF offices in New York City, a bronze statue called *Spirit of Audrey* honors her selfless work and generous spirit.

Even though she had a painful childhood, Audrey used her pain to be the best mother to her children and to reach out and help other children around the world.

66 When things get worse, we need each other more. 99

Audrey becomes a UNICEF Goodwill Ambassador. **1988**

Audrey goes to Ethiopia. **1988**

Audrey goes to Somalia. **1992**

Audrey receives the Presidential Medal of Freedom. **1992**

Audrey dies. **1993**

# CHAPTER 8

# SO . . . WHO WAS AUDREY HEPBURN ?

# ✦ Challenge Accepted! ✦

Now that you have learned about Audrey Hepburn's life as a dancer, actress, and humanitarian, let's test your new knowledge in a little "who, what, when, where, why, and how" quiz. Feel free to look back in the text to find the answers if you need to, but try to remember first!

**1** **When was Audrey born?**

→ A  1944
→ B  1929
→ C  1993
→ D  1960

**2** **Who were Audrey's half brothers?**
→ A  Mel and Andrea
→ B  Alex and Sean
→ C  Ian and Alex
→ D  Sean and Luca

**3** What country invaded the
Netherlands during World War II?

→ A Germany

→ B Holland

→ C England

→ D United States

**4** Who told Audrey she couldn't be a
prima ballerina?

→ A Her mother

→ B Her father

→ C Her ballet teacher

→ D Her husband

**5** What last name did Audrey
drop to make her stage name?

→ A Ferrer

→ B Hepburn

→ C van Heemstra

→ D Ruston

### 6 Why did Audrey go to the New York City?

→ A  To be in a TV show
→ B  To be in a play
→ C  To be in a movie
→ D  To be a ballerina

### 7 What movie did Audrey win an Oscar for?

→ A  *Gigi*
→ B  *Breakfast at Tiffany's*
→ C  *Roman Holiday*
→ D  *My Fair Lady*

### 8 How did Audrey help hungry children?

→ A  She traveled to war-torn countries
→ B  She raised money to buy food
→ C  She worked for UNICEF
→ D  All of the above

**9** **When did Audrey have her first child, Sean?**

→ A 1970

→ B 1960

→ C 1959

→ D 1988

**10** **Where did Audrey go on her last UNICEF trip?**

→ A Somalia

→ B Switzerland

→ C Ethiopia

→ D Guatemala

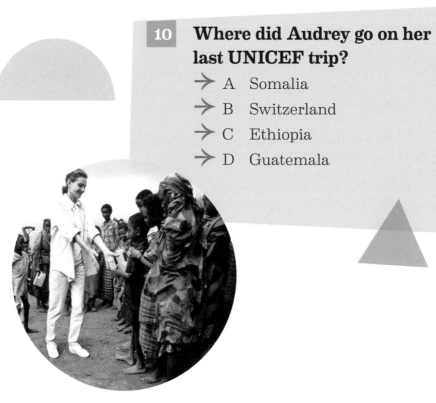

# ✦ Our World ✦

How did Audrey affect our world today? Let's look at a few things that happened because of Audrey Hepburn.

→ Audrey was an ambassador for UNICEF. She helped the organization grow and raised money to help the world's children. Today, her granddaughter, Emma Kathleen Hepburn Ferrer, also works with UNICEF.

→ Fashion designer Hubert de Givenchy worked with Audrey for most of her life and helped to create her famous look. Audrey showed women they could look comfortable and beautiful at the same time, and her style is still considered iconic today.

→ Audrey died of a rare cancer of the appendix called pseudomyxoma peritonei (SOO-doh-mik-SOH-muh PAYR-ih-TOH-ny). Her son Sean is a patron of Pseudomyxoma Survivor, a group that helps people with the same disease. He is also an ambassador for Rare Disease Day (February 28). Today there is a better chance of a cure thanks to people like Sean who help raise money and awareness.

JUMP
—IN THE—
THINK
TANK
FOR

—MORE!—

Now let's think more about what Audrey Hepburn did to be a role model for others.

→ Audrey was a role model for young people because she was kind, brave, and good to children. Who is your role model? Why?

→ Audrey had a terrible fear of public speaking, so she practiced her lines and speeches over and over again. What is your fear, and what can you do to face it?

→ Audrey went to war-torn countries to save starving children. What could you do to help people in need?

# Glossary

**Allied:** Troops from different countries that work together in war. In WWII, the Allied countries were Great Britain, the United States, France, and, later, the Soviet Union.

**ambassador:** A person who represents an organization and campaigns for a cause.

**asthma:** A condition that affects the airways and causes breathing problems.

**audition:** A show of skills to try to get a role or job as a singer, actor, dancer, or musician.

**baroness:** A woman who is a member of the nobility and ranks high in society.

**cabaret:** Entertainment or shows held in a nightclub.

**chorus girl:** A young woman who sings and dances as part of a group in a musical.

**Congress:** The legislative branch of the federal government that represents the American people and makes the nation's laws. It shares power with the executive branch, led by the president, and the judicial branch, whose highest body is the Supreme Court of the United States.

**depression:** A major drop in business and spending.

**dictator**: A ruler with complete power over a country.

**director**: A person who is in charge of making a movie.

**Dutch Underground**: People from the Netherlands who set up networks to help the Allies.

**elegant**: Graceful and stylish.

**genre**: A type of art—such as film, music, or writing—that has a common style or form.

**humanitarian**: A person or thing that betters people's lives.

**icon**: Someone who is widely known, influential, and makes an important impact on society.

**influencer**: A person who changes the behavior or thoughts of others.

**legend**: A person who is very famous and well-liked.

**Nazis**: Members of a German political party led by Adolf Hitler that controlled Germany from 1933 to 1945.

**nominated**: Chosen as a candidate to receive an award.

**orphanage**: A home for children in need.

**playbill:** A booklet handed out at a theater that lists the cast and crew for the show being performed.

**prima ballerina:** The lead dancer in a ballet.

**producer:** A person who makes a movie or play.

**project:** To make your voice reach into an audience.

**Resistance:** A secret group that goes against those in charge of a country.

**retired:** Finished working in a certain career.

**scholarship:** Money used to support a student's education, often awarded for good grades or skills.

**UNICEF:** Stands for United Nations International Emergency Fund, an organization that helps children who are victims of war.

**vaccine:** A treatment that helps to protect people from disease.

# Bibliography

Cardillo, Margaret. *Just Being Audrey*. Illustrated by Julia Denos. New York: Balzer + Bray, 2011.

Coan, Helena, director. *Audrey*. Salon Pictures and XYZ Films, 2020. 1 hr., 40 min. https://www.netflix.com/title/81354558.

Ferrer, Sean Hepburn. *Audrey Hepburn, An Elegant Spirit*. New York: Atria Books, 2003.

Ferrer, Sean Hepburn, and Katherine Hepburn Ferrer. *Little Audrey's Daydream*. Illustrated by Dominique Corbasson and François Avril. New York: Princeton Architectural Press, 2020.

Matzen, Robert. *Dutch Girl: Audrey Hepburn and World War II*. Pittsburgh: GoodKnight Books, 2019.

Matzen, Robert. *Warrior: Audrey Hepburn*. Pittsburgh: GoodKnight Books, 2021.

Soto, Donald. *Enchantment: The Life of Audrey Hepburn*. New York: Harmony Books, 2006.

UNICEF. "Audrey Hepburn." Accessed October 28, 2023. https://www .unicef.org/goodwill-ambassadors/audrey-hepburn.

# About the Author

**Natasha Wing** has been writing children's books for more than 30 years. She has written biographies about Eliza Hamilton and Jackie Kennedy Onassis. Natasha was named after a character in the book *War and Peace* by Leo Tolstoy. Audrey Hepburn played the role of Natasha in the 1956 movie *War and Peace*.

# About the Illustrator

**Marta Dorado** is a full-time freelance illustrator born in Gijón (Asturias, Spain) in 1989 and raised in a nearby village. She attended university in Pamplona, where she still lives, and started a career as a graphic designer in the advertising industry. Marta's childhood, surrounded by nature and close to the sea, strongly influences her work.

# WHO WILL INSPIRE YOU NEXT?

EXPLORE A WORLD OF HEROES AND ROLE MODELS IN
**THE STORY OF** ...AN INSPIRING BIOGRAPHY SERIES
FOR YOUNG READERS.

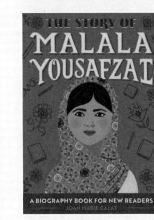

### → LOOK FOR THIS SERIES ←
WHEREVER BOOKS AND EBOOKS ARE SOLD